WIDE CONTRASTS IN THE SCENERY OF SCOTLAND ALWAYS IMPRESS THE VISITOR. WHERE ELSE CAN BE FOUND IN SO SMALL AN AREA MOUNTAINS, SAVAGE SEAS, ROUGH COASTS, WOODED VALLEYS, WILD MOORLAND, TUMBLING RIVERS AND FERTILE PLAINS? CHANGING PLAY OF LIGHT BROUGHT BY THE FICKLE CLIMATE ADDS MYSTERY TO THE SCOTTISH EXPERIENCE.

NO-ONE IN RECENT YEARS HAS CAPTURED THIS EVER-CHANGING VARIETY AS SENSITIVELY AS THE PHOTOGRAPHER, COLIN BAXTER, WHO HAS IN THIS SERIES SELECTED CERTAIN AREAS AND THEMES TO CONVEY THE RICH DIVERSITY OF SCOTLAND'S CITIES AND COUNTRYSIDE.

MOST ASPECTS OF SCOTLAND'S SCENERY CAN BE FOUND ON THE ISLE OF MULL FROM THE BASALT CLIFFS OF CARSAIG AND THE PEAK OF BEN MORE IN THE SOUTH TO THE SWEEPING MACHAIR OF CALGARY TO THE NORTH AND THE PAINTED HOUSES CIRCLING TOBERMORY HARBOUR.

THE LONG DESERTED ROSS OF MULL LEADS TO FIONNPHORT FOR THE SHORT CROSSING TO ST. COLUMBA'S IONA. THE BURIAL PLACE OF THE KINGS OF SCOTLAND LIES IN THE SHADOW OF THE MAGNIFICENT ABBEY, BOTH CONVEYING A POWERFUL SENSE OF HISTORY AND TRANQUILLITY.

CRUACHAN BEAG

·MULL AND IONA·

COLIN BAXTER

RICHARD DREW PUBLISHING
GLASGOW

Eorsa,
Loch na Keal

OVERLEAF:
Loch Scridain

DUART CASTLE

IONA ABBEY

IONA ABBEY

LOWER ARDTUN

SUNSET OVER IONA

Loch na Keal

Kilfinichen Bay

SOUND OF MULL
AND MAOL NAN UAN

River Ba

FACING PAGE:
GLAC AN LIR

Druim Dhughaill,
Iona

Loch Beg

Near Fionnphort

Stac an Aoineidh,
Iona

LOBSTER AND
PRAWN CREELS

FISHERMAN'S COTTAGE
NEAR FANMORE

TOBERMORY

GRULINE

LOCH SCRIDAIN

FACING PAGE:
CREAG MHOR
AND
INCH KENNETH

LOCH POIT NA H-I,
ROSS OF MULL

OVERLEAF:
GOMETRA
WITH STAFFA
IN THE DISTANCE

MAOL NAN UAN

BEN MORE
IN WINTER

BEN MORE
FROM NEAR SALEN

BEINN MHEADHOIN
AND
BEINN THUNICARAIDH

Post Box,
Knock   Iona Post Office

TIRORAN
POST OFFICE

OVERLEAF:
DUSK,
LOCH NA KEAL

BAC MOR
(DUTCHMAN'S CAP)

DUN BHIORAMUILL,
ULVA

RUBHA NA MOINE,
LOCH NA KEAL

First Published 1986 by
RICHARD DREW PUBLISHING
6 CLAIRMONT GARDENS, GLASGOW, G3 7LW, SCOTLAND

Printed and bound in Great Britain by
Blantyre Printing and Binding Co. Ltd.

British Library Cataloguing in Publication Data

"Mull and Iona — (Experience Scotland)
1. Iona (Scotland) — Description and
travel — Guide-books 2. Mull, Island
of (Scotland) — Description and travel
— Guide-books
I. Title   II. Series
914.14'23   DA880.17

ISBN 0-86267-154-X